Write Fast Earn Fast!

*Write and Sell Content
In the Same Day*

RON KNESS

No part of this book may be reproduced, stored in a retrieval system, or transmitted in any form or by any means, electronic, mechanical, photocopying, recording, scanning, or otherwise, without the prior written permission of the publisher, except for the inclusion of brief quotations in a review.

This book is for **personal use only**.

Copyright © 2016 Ron Kness

All rights reserved.

ISBN-13: 978-1537680583

ISBN-10: 1537680587

Contents

Disclaimer 4

Introduction 5

There Are Many Ways to Earn Money from Writing 8

Finding a Profitable Niche 10

Profitable Writing Ideas 12

Offer Your Services as a Freelancer 21

Mindset & Goals 23

How to Write 5,000 Words in 3 Hours 26

Final Thoughts 30

About the Author 31

Disclaimer

This guide has been written for information purposes only. Every effort has been made to make this guide as complete and accurate as possible. However, there may be mistakes in typography or content. Also, this guide provides information only up to the publishing date. Therefore, use it as a guide and not as the ultimate source.

The purpose of this guide is to educate. The author and the publisher does not warrant that the information contained in this guide is fully complete and shall not be responsible for any errors or omissions. The author and publisher shall have neither liability nor responsibility to any person or entity with respect to any loss or damage caused or alleged to be caused directly or indirectly by this guide.

Introduction

Can you write an information product and sell it within 24 hours? Of course you can-- I've done it many times. The only thing standing in your way is your mindset. Mindset, along with goals, are covered later in this guide where you'll see why both are important to your writing **and** selling.

The bottom line is if you want to earn from your writing, you can. That is the marketing side of this business and the less exciting part to many people. Fast, slow, a little or a lot, if you want to make money from writing, it all starts with first having a written product to sell.

The voice in your head tells you that you have to toil and stress over your writing before you're "allowed" to earn from it is totally wrong. Write it and sell it! The time spent writing doesn't necessarily equate to more money. After all the only thing you are really selling is time, so the faster you can write, the more you can sell, thus increasing your rate per hour.

Money loves speed

Everyone is an expert at something. If you can write about a solution you found to a problem that other people are experiencing, there is an audience out there that will love your content. In fact, they're waiting for your content right now; all you have to do is find them. You can really help people if you write on hot topics and release your content quickly.

Once you find that audience, it's a win-win, of course. You get to earn money quickly and you get to serve your audience at the same time.

And if you deliver what you promised, they will buy again and again and ... they will be loyal customers for a long time.

What do you do if you don't have an audience? No worries... you can find a fantastic niche (or service) and still put this method to use.

Note: depending on how you go about things, it *might* take you longer than 24 hours to see those first profits. But it IS possible. Absolutely. I'm living proof!

You'll have to work hard on getting eyeballs on all these new offers you'll be putting out there. But I know you can do it from the information in this guide.

Content - especially written content delivered digitally - is what the Internet thrives on. People love to learn things. They read blogs, websites, reports, guides, books ... everything. And webmasters constantly need information to post on their blogs and websites. Some of the information they will write, but some they will buy. If they need what you write, and your quality is high and it is priced right, they will gladly trade dollars for time and buy your content.

There are certain markets that buy new content and how-to's all the time. Yes, the business-to-business niche is one that has customers who tend to buy frequently, and because they are in a business themselves, tend to have the money to buy.

But there are definitely other niches where you can profit quickly. Build a list in sub-niches of parenting, self-help, motivation, fitness, health, relationships like dating, and so on, and you can do well.

You can write something people in your market will eat up and buy like crazy... and you can do it in a day.

There are some people who think that your writing isn't worth anything if you didn't spend weeks, months, or even years on it. They scoff at the idea that anything created in 24 hours can be valuable. But how will they know how little time you pent writing if you don't tell them. And honestly, it isn't important. As long as your product is factual and well written, it doesn't matter how much (or little) time it took to write it.

That's totally false. The more you write, the faster you'll get at writing. And we're not talking about super-long books or pieces here. We're talking about short, inexpensive, fantastically helpful and valuable content that your audience will love.

Don't listen to the naysayers who tell you that you can't do this. You can do this. I do it all the time and have done so for years.

There Are Many Ways to Earn Money from Writing

There are actually many different ways you can earn from your writing in just 24 hours. You don't have to put yourself in a box, although with that said, there is some merit to specializing in certain niches and even certain types of information formats. I, for instance like to write and self-publish books about health and fitness. However each month I commercially write health and fitness articles for a writer in England; each week write a column for a specialized job search website. I occasionally also write longer pieces for a website management company on education – in the 3,000 to 4,000 word range.

In the beginning, I think you'll find that you want to try many different methods, like blog posts, reports, articles, and books. With some experience, you'll start to mix and match, find what you like to write and come up with great ideas for earning on your own.

You can also look at the written assets you already own. Figure out how you can earn even more money from those assets. It is called repurposing and is one key to making as much as you can from one writing.

For example, can you combine a group of similar articles or blog posts to create a guide you can sell?

Can you break a large report or guide down that you've written and turn it into PLR (Private Label Rights) list builders, blog posts, articles or something else?

Let the ideas come to you as you go through this guide. Take notes on what you think will work best for you. You'll want to tuck some of these ideas away for later. You'll want to use others right away.

Finding a Profitable Niche

I really want to emphasize this because it's so important. You really have to choose a niche people are already spending a lot of money in.

Don't just choose a niche you are interested in, without doing some market research on that niche, and expect to earn great money -- it can happen that way, but usually doesn't.

Find a niche that has a lot of chatter about it online. It should have Facebook pages and groups dedicated to it. It should have dedicated forums. There should already be hot products on that topic that are selling like crazy.

Do some digging and make sure there's traffic and money flowing around your chosen niche. Those elements must be there or there's no chance of you earning money from your writing within 24 hours.

Note: You won't hit it out of the park every time, even when you do your research. Sometimes you'll be shocked at how much you earn with something you created quickly. Other times you'll be disappointed.

But all the while, you're building up assets and earning fast and snowballing your earnings and business into something incredible.

I'm not going to tell you exactly how you should structure and run your business. I'm going to give you ideas for how you can tackle a great and profitable niche (like business-to-business-Internet Marketing) with your writing and earn from it very quickly.

Next, I'll go through each of the ways you might earn from your writing in as little as a day. I'll go more in depth about these methods a bit further on in this guide.

Profitable Writing Ideas

There are so many ways to make money from writing, I don't know where to begin. Here are five ways that you can use to kick out writing products quickly and paid just as fast.

Write and Release a Report For Sale in 24 Hours

One way you can earn money from your writing in 24 hours is by writing a quick report. Maybe you've noticed a hot trend in your niche and you want to tackle some issue or solve some problem in that niche right away.

For example, one of the recent niches to take off like crazy was Pokemon GO. That seem to explode overnight! People created content for that niche almost immediately -- and those who got there first, tended to do best. But even now, you can still sell content in this niche and probably will be able to well into the near-term future.

On a topic you know well, you can write a report of around 3,000-5,000 words in a day. You'll be able to write more words per day (and per hour) as you get more experience.

You'll write the report and put it up for sale - at a price your market will support and that reflects a fair price based on the length and/or helpfulness of the guide. Now let's go more in depth about how you can write and release a report for sale within 24 hours.

First, you'll need a hot topic within your niche. Go with something trending and that's already earning money.

If you're sure it is a niche/sub-niche/genre that WILL earn money, go ahead and get in front of the trend.

Examine the reports and guides that are already out on the topic. How can you target a very small sub-niche within a larger niche in a way that's proven to sell, but also takes a unique angle or slant to the issue?

Find your angle and then move ahead.

You might want to take some time as you're preparing to write to contact affiliates who might promote your report as soon as it's released. Is there a topic they would like to see a written report on? Many affiliates only sell other people's products for a commission, but don't actually write anything themselves. This is especially important to do if you don't currently have your own list and plan to sell through affiliates.

Promise those potential affiliates a review copy as soon as it's finished. Talk up the profit potential and the fact that you'll offer a great commission, via a sales platform like JVZoo.

Then, do your research and outlining. Make sure you're focusing on that unique angle that will set your report apart from the others that are out there.

Write your heart out once everything is organized and ready to go! Now edit and proofread.

Save your report as a PDF, upload it, and give your affiliates a URL where they can go and get their affiliate link. That way any sales they make through their link are credited to them and they will get the commission from those sales.

One good place to list your reports for sale is JVZoo. You'll need to create a sales page for your report.

You can model this after other similar reports and products that are out there -- but of course you'll want to tailor yours to make it unique to your product.

Once your report is finished and listed, start driving traffic to your sales page. One quick way that costs nothing is to do a Facebook post to groups in your niche. I've gotten sales in less than an hour after posting.

You will also want to get more affiliates on board. Strive to make a list of 100 affiliates you can contact for promotion over the coming days.

You can absolutely make your first sale within 24 hours. And you should be connecting sales of your product to your autoresponder account (like Aweber or GetResponse). Every customer should be added to your email list. Of course you can manually add them to your list or use the opt-in features of your autoresponder program that will automatically add them to your list. And that list is valuable as you will use it over and over to contact customers that have bought from you before when you have a new product in their niche of interest.

Write and Release PLR for Sale in 24 Hours

If you're writing content to sell to business owners, you can certainly earn within 24 hours. Let's say you see a great niche business owners are targeting like crazy. You know the topic is really profitable for these business owners.

You can write content and sell it to them with Private Label Rights. They get to use the content for their business.

You'll sell this content over and over again - each buyer will personalize the content to suit their specific needs so there usually isn't any exact duplication.

You can sell PLR articles, reports, guides, etc. When you write and release PLR for sale, you're creating something for other business owners to use to improve their business. It's PLR, so they get to buy great content for around $1.00 per 400-word page that didn't cost you anything to write except time. And you get to sell the content over and over again to different business owners, so it's a win-win.

To create an article pack of PLR, focus on topics business owners might want to use for article marketing, email marketing, and/or for as posts for their blogs.

As noted, you typically might want to initially price article packs at $1 per article. Then based on what other PLR sellers are doing with similar packs, adjust your prices and pack content accordingly.

Contact others who sell PLR packs. Offer them a look at the articles. See if they will promote the pack for you as an affiliate to their customer list. As with the articles, offer them a great commission, and list on a sales platform like JVZoo so it will easily manage your affiliates, sales, and delivery. ClickBank is another good marketplace platform with good affiliate support.

Always connect sales of each pack to your autoresponder so you capture the email addresses of all those who buy from you. That way, you can email your own list the next time you have a PLR pack for sale.

Autoresponders allow you to segment your list which is breaking down your total list into smaller lists. For example your buyers of PLR could be different than your buyers of non-PLR. You can set up your autoresponcder so that each segment get the information applicable just to them.

Contact business owners, those with a similar niche site -- basically, get the word out wherever you can think of, where business owners will be interested in buying an article pack on the topic you've targeted.

The same applies for PLR reports, books, blog posts and autoresponder content. Get affiliates on board-- both those who sell their own PLR (because they have their own lists of targeted buyers) and business owners with interested lists.

Where can you find these affiliates? JVZoo allows affiliates to apply to promote your product. You can contact those with similar packs for sale. And you can find affiliates and JV networks on Facebook groups, etc.

Note that many affiliates look for offers that have a front and back end offer, so you might make more sales all the way around this way. A back end offer is an offer a buyer receives after buying your initial offer. It is typically priced higher than the initial offer, and may have a down sell to it, which is the back end offer scaled down in size and offered at a price less than the full back end price. If they don't take the first upsell, they sometimes will take the down sell.

Typically the initial offer is commissioned at 100% with follow-on OTOs (One-Time Offers) commissioned at around 50%. While you don't make any money on the frontend, you do on the more expensive back end.

These follow-on offers usually occur between the buy and delivery of the product, however they can also be presented as emails sent from your autoresponder at certain intervals after the initial sale.

I can't stress this enough -- always attach sales of your product to your autoresponder list so that you're building a list with every sale. Building your list is even more important than earning money within the first 24 hours! Your list will give you future security and ensure that you can always make sales within 24 hours (or even immediately) from everything you write from on forward.

Do Both

You can also choose to do both! Let's say there's a great, hot niche in the business or Internet marketing world. You can write a report or guide on that topic. You can then can either sell the guide whole or break it down into articles as PLR and sell to those buyers.

You can create content that suits both purposes in a short amount of time. Some will just want the guide you've created for personal use, while others will want the PLR so they can modify and use the content in their business. The difference is the non-PLR (report or guide) doesn't have an editable source file with it and is usually in PDF format. PLR on the other hand is in either Word or plain text which of course are source files and may be edited.

This an example where the PLR could be a back end offer and either more or less expensive than the guide. The PLR could be a collection of content different from what is in the guide that the buyer could use to help sell the guide, such as articles that could be posted to a blog post whose intent is to sell the guide (if the terms in your license provided with each product allows buyers to sell the content as their own. Some allow "for personal use only" in which the product cannot be resold).

This can work very well! JVZoo allows you to very easily offer upsells, downsells and even bonuses provided by the affiliate themselves if the customer buys from them. You'll have to create sales pages for both the front end product as well as the PLR upsell or follow-on content.

Write and Release 'One-Person' Articles for Sale

This is another idea that targets business owners. Business owners know that they need content in order to boost their business. You can write an article pack that targets a great topic you know business owners will definitely want.

You'll then advertise and sell these articles to just one person. They will get the sole rights to the content, so you can (and should) charge more. This is different than offering PLR to the articles, where you'd sell the rights to many business owners instead of one, hence the reason for the higher price – you only have an opportunity to sell this work once.

With PLR, you'd price the article pack quite low so many can buy it. With one-person rights, you'd price the article pack much higher because you are only selling it once.

It's sort of ready-to-go ghostwritten content. A business can use it but doesn't have to edit it much if at all, because they are assured no other business will be buying the same content. Constant Content was an example of a company that sold articles and content in this way.

You can contact your clients once you've written this article pack. Or you can contact business owners you know might be interested.

For this type of content, you won't really want affiliates for this sort of offer -- but you might joint venture with someone who may have more contacts that you have to actually help make the sale. You can do the same thing with reports, books or most digital content you write.

Advertise the content for sale as ghostwriting they don't have to wait for. It's really appealing for many business owners to have something that's ready to go.

If you target the right audience, you can absolutely sell your book within a day. Price it right and write it fast!

PLR and Other Methods of Using Ready Content to Earn

What if you're not really "a writer" or you're still really intimidated by the thought of writing 4,000-5,000 words in a day? That's okay... you can ease your way in.

Find a PLR offer that allows you to resell it. Take the day to modify that content to suit your exact audience. Generally speaking, you have to rewrite at least 50% of the original content in order to sell it again as PLR.

That is usually easily done by changing the slant of the original content, adding a paragraph at the beginning and end, and maybe changing a few things in the middle such as adding or deleting content. Rewording the title too is usually a good idea.

Put it up for sale, get affiliates on board, and drive traffic to that offer in any way you can. You can use JVZoo for this content just as you could if you'd written it entirely on your own.

Indeed, just as you can start offering your own PLR for sale, you can buy and modify the PLR of others and put it up for sale yourself. Just be sure to work within the limits of the license provided with the original content.

You can also hire writers to custom-create content for you. The site Fiverr and Upwork are good sites to find a writer at reasonable rates. They'll write it and you'll sell it! Although the profit margin is usually much less because you have to pay the writer.

The point is, don't think you have to be a world-class and super-quick writer right away. You can earn from writing within 24 hours by having others do the heavy lifting for you.

Offer Your Services as a Freelancer

One of the fastest ways you can earn from your writing within 24 hours is to offer your services to a business owner as a ghostwriter or work-for-hire agreement.

There are many businesses out there that hire freelancers. They often need a lot of content that they don't have time to write themselves.

Advertise that you're available to write fantastic content. You can get orders very quickly and earn money as a freelancer within 24 hours if you go about this in the right way.

This is the reverse of the methods we've talked about so far. You'll offer your services first and write later. You'll need a sample of your writing that you can use to showcase your writing skills. Put your writing sample on your website or blog that offers your services. You can offer articles, reports, guides, sales copy, etc.

Make the ordering process as simple as possible. The easier, the more orders you'll get.

How do you set yourself apart from other freelancers out there? Make it clear why people should hire you over others, especially if you're new. If you have made sales before as a service provider, garnish a testimonial or two and post to your website as well.

One way, if you're new and want to make faster sales, is to offer a grand-opening special. You can also offer a discount, a free pack of content or maybe a discount on future purchase.

You are only limited by your imagination. Take a look at successful freelancers to see how they do it!

Then, advertise that you're open for business. Find business owners/Internet marketers who might be interested in your services. Contact other freelance writers to see if they have overflow work.

Take a look at a service like Upwork to see if there are jobs there that you'd like to apply for.

In the beginning, you'll spend time networking and getting clients. But if you put your offer in front of the right eyeballs, you can absolutely launch your freelancing business within 24 hours and earn within a day.

Mindset & Goals

Mindset

As you might have guessed, you have to have the right mindset if you're going to be able to earn money within 24 hours.

Do you think you can do it?

If not, why not?

Maybe you've thought your whole life that earning money from writing had to be hard and take forever. Maybe you're just not used to the Internet culture of money loving speed.

If something is helpful to the buyer and totally satisfies them, does it matter how long it took for you to create it? Of course not. What matters is that they got their money's worth or even more than their money's worth and that you made a sale. Always over deliver!

I promise you there are writers and product creators who consistently produce high quality content at lightning speeds.

There are business owners and Internet marketers who take an idea and turn it into cash within 24 hours-- and they aren't any more talented or skilled than you are. They just took action, made it their goal, and crushed it!

Do yourself a favor - get into the mindset that will allow you to earn from your writing quickly. You can do it. With more and more practice, you can rinse and repeat to do it whenever you need or want to accomplish.

Goals

It's important to have goals for everything you do in life and being in business is no different. If you don't have a goal, you're not nearly as likely to follow through and succeed.

Let's say you know that you want to launch your services as a freelance writer... someday. But how do you know when that "someday" has arrived?

But when are you actually going to do it? (January 1, 2017?) How much are you going to earn from it? ($1,000, $5,000, ??) How long will it take you to earn money? (24 hours, a week, a month, ??)

I've given you a goal right here in this guide. You're going to launch your freelance writing services and earn from it within 24 hours. Maybe you'll set your monetary goal at earning your first, fast $50. You can do it! I have several times over.

Maybe freelancing isn't for you. But you know that there are tons of business owners who are crazy for PLR because it really helps them in their business. So, you know that you want to start selling PLR ... someday.

But someday isn't going to earn you money. Make it your goal to either buy or write a PLR report and earn from it-- even your first $5-- within 24 hours.

As you can see, it's important to make your goals solid and actionable. They should be specific. You're going to write SOMETHING or launch SOMETHING and earn SOMETHING from it within 24 hours.

Can you really do this? Yes, you can. Believe in yourself. And you'll just get better and better and faster and faster over time.

Prove it to yourself by taking action immediately!

How to Write 5,000 Words in 3 Hours

Before we go any further, I want to make it clear to you that you can write a seemingly huge amount in a short amount of time.

If you had to guess, how long would it take you to write 5,000 words? Did you know that some writers can write this amount in 3 hours or less?

Do you think you can write 5,000 words in 3 hours? Maybe not in the beginning, but eventually you'll get there.

And 5,000 words is absolutely an amount you can profit from, quite quickly ... our focus is on you earning money from around 5,000 words or so, within 24 hours. In reality much fewer words can earn you money. A pack of 5 PLR articles at 400 words apiece is only 2,000 words and you can easily knock that out in less than a day even when first starting out.

Outlining

One of the most important things you can do to ensure you're able to write 5,000 words in 3 hours (or 5 or 10 or whatever you're setting as your goal for now), is to outline.

You shouldn't have to think about what's coming next while you write!

Outline and plan exactly what's going to go into your written content before you start writing.

What are your major chapters, titles, or topics?

What are your sub-topics?

Figure this out and organize it in a way that works for you. The more detailed, the better (but don't spend a lot of time doing this). I know, flashbacks from your school outlining days, but it is still the method I use today.

Researching

Do your research ahead of time as well. Pop your research right where it belongs within your outline. Cite sources where you need to and make sure you're going with sources you know are correct-- cross reference sources. I like to see the same information in at least two different sources. However with PLR, sources are not usually noted. With ghostwriting, the customer may or may not want cited sources. Be sure to ask before writing so you can capture the sources at the time of research.

You want to be known for having the very best information and research in your writing.

Your outline and your research should be thoroughly organized (introduction, body points, and conclusion), before you actually get started writing. You should be able to fly through your writing once it's all organized like this. This known as free writing because you are just getting words on paper, albeit virtually, without regard to grammar or punctuation. After writing you can go back through it and edit for these things, along with clarity.

Focusing

If you want to earn a lot from your writing, you really need to focus. You shouldn't be flipping back and forth with social media and this, that, and the other. As a matter-of-fact, close all browser tabs except the ones directly tied to what you are writing.

Focus! Turn off the distractions and the notifications. You have your outline and research ready to go. You just need to lock yourself in your office, get in the zone and write. This will allow you to write more quickly than you ever thought possible.

Dictating

If you're a very slow typist, you might want to consider using a voice-recognition software program like DragonNaturallySpeaking to dictate your writing. You can speak much more quickly than you can type!

Google Docs also has built in dictation now! If you have a newer computer and/or operating system, your computer probably has built in dictation.

Note that you'll probably have to edit for mis-heard words and things like punctuation and grammar ... but it's not out of the question that you could dictate 5,000 words in 90 minutes or so, and then edit those words over the next 90 minutes.

Yes, it's fast. And it's possible.

Obviously don't rush things if it's going to affect your quality. It should always be quality over quantity, but once you get some experience under your belt you can deliver both equally well, But if you're well organized and focused, you WILL have fantastic quality even though you're writing/dictating incredibly quickly.

Editing

You'll definitely want to edit what you write -- whether you've typed it out or dictated. Sure, you might still have an error here and there. But read through, proofread, and edit through a few times to make your work the best it can be.

This isn't about perfectionism, though. Even heavily edited books that are sold by the big five publishing houses still contain errors! Don't let perfectionism paralyze your production, You have to know when good enough is good enough.

Final Thoughts

Yes, you can write and earn within 24 hours. You can't snap your fingers and have the writing done. You're going to have to push through and get it done, get your sales page up, and get eyeballs on your offer.

But you can do it -- whether you're new or experienced!

Many have done it before you. And, as you build your list and get faster at writing, it will get easier every single time ... and more profitable.

It starts with a single step. Choose how you're going to earn with your writing within the next day and get to it!

I believe in you. You have what it takes. I can't wait to hear about your success story.

About the Author

I grew up in Central Minnesota, where my parents owned and operated a fishing resort. Once out of high school I tried a couple of semesters of college, only to quit halfway through the Spring term; I decided at that time that college wasn't for me.

Then I decided to follow my father's previous occupation as an auto mechanic. I graduated from a two-year of vocational training course and worked as a mechanic for five years. While in vocational training, I decided to join the National Guard where I eventually ended up working full-time for 32 years.

So how does all of this relate to writing? In one of my leadership schools, the instructor, who was an English teacher at a juvenile detention center, presented writing to me in a whole new way - a way that started to develop my interest in working with words.

I eventually went back to college on the GI Bill while I was working and earned my Bachelor's degree in Business Administration. Taking a class or two per semester at night and on weekends took me seven years to complete my degree.

Fast forward about 40 years and I now have published over 75 books on Amazon for Kindle, CreateSpace and other publishing platforms.

Besides my own writing, I also ghostwrite ebooks, reports, articles, blogs and do Kindle conversions for clients on a variety of topics.

Today my wife and I are retired from our careers and live in Gold Canyon, AZ. I now write as a retirement business where you'll find me happily sitting in my office typing away on my laptop as I work on my next book or ghostwriting project... that is if we are not traveling on a cruise ship - our new-found mode of travel.

www.ingramcontent.com/pod-product-compliance
Lightning Source LLC
Chambersburg PA
CBHW021450170526
45164CB00001B/454